Colorado's Fourteeners — By the Numbers

Front Range

Grays Peak	14,270
Torreys Peak	14,267
Mount Evans	14,264
Longs Peak	14,255
Pikes Peak	14,110
Mount Bierstadt	14,060

Mosquito Range

Mount Lincoln	14,286
Mount Bross	14,172
Mount Democrat	14,148
Mount Sherman	14,036

Tenmile Range

Quandary Peak	14,265

Sawatch Range

Mount Elbert	14,433
Mount Massive	14,421
Mount Harvard	14,420
La Plata Peak	14,336
Mount Antero	14,269
Mount Shavano	14,229
Mount Belford	14,197
Mount Princeton	14,197
Mount Yale	14,196
Tabeguache Peak	14,155
Mount Oxford	14,153
Mount Columbia	14,073
Missouri Mountain	14,067
Mount of the Holy Cross	14,005
Huron Peak	14,003

Sangre de Cristo Range

Blanca Peak	14,345
Crestone Peak	14,294
Crestone Needle	14,197
Kit Carson Mountain	14,165
Humboldt Peak	14,064
Ellingwood Point	14,042
Mount Lindsey	14,042
Little Bear Peak	14,037

Culebra Range

Culebra Peak	14,047

Elk Mountains

Castle Peak	14,265
Maroon Peak	14,156
Capitol Peak	14,130
Snowmass Mountain	14,092
Pyramid Peak	14,018
North Maroon Peak	14,014

San Juan Mountains

Uncompahgre Peak	14,309
Handies Peak	14,048
Redcloud Peak	14,034
Wetterhorn Peak	14,015
Sunshine Peak	14,001

San Miguel Mountains

Mount Wilson	14,246
El Diente Peak	14,159
Wilson Peak	14,017

Sneffels Range

Mount Sneffels	14,150

Needle Mountains

Mount Eolus	14,083
Windom Peak	14,082
Sunlight Peak	14,059

La Garita Mountains

San Luis Peak	14,014

14,000 FEET

A CELEBRATION OF COLORADO'S HIGHEST MOUNTAINS

WALTER R. BORNEMAN & TODD CAUDLE

with DAVE SHOWALTER & DAVID ANSCHICKS

Published by

SKYLINE PRESS
Pueblo, Colorado

14,000 FEET

A CELEBRATION OF COLORADO'S HIGHEST MOUNTAINS

by WALTER R. BORNEMAN & TODD CAUDLE

with DAVE SHOWALTER & DAVID ANSCHICKS

Published by
Skyline Press
P. O. Box 371
Pueblo, Colorado 81002
Second Printing

Copy-editing by
Deb Acord
Jacket design by
Moira Dyer, Olson/Kotowski, Inc.
Redondo Beach, California
Map by
Michael Borop, World Sites Atlas
Special thanks to
Kristy Judd, Executive Director of the
Colorado Mountain Club

All historic photos are property of the
Colorado Mountain Club,
used by permission

Back cover, left: Blanca and Ellingwood rise above the Huerfano River
Back cover, top-right: Longs Peak at sunset
Back cover, bottom-right: CMC outing, Chicago Basin, circa 1937
Right: The San Miguel massif from Bolam Pass

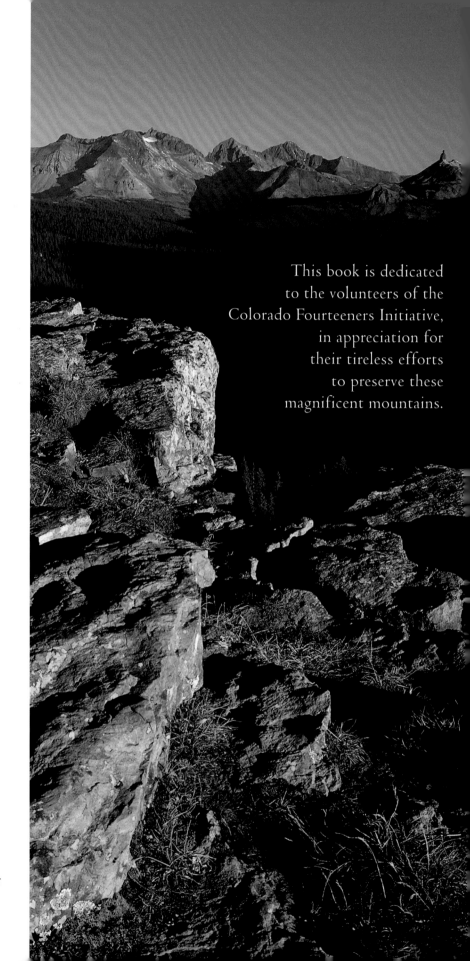

This book is dedicated
to the volunteers of the
Colorado Fourteeners Initiative,
in appreciation for
their tireless efforts
to preserve these
magnificent mountains.

TABLE OF CONTENTS

Two centuries ago while Lewis and Clark explored the Missouri River, another young army officer, Lieutenant Zebulon Montgomery Pike, was tasked with probing the southern extremes of the newly acquired Louisiana Territory. In July 1806, 27-year-old Pike departed Fort Bellefontaine near St. Louis in command of 22 men. His orders were straightforward: follow the Arkansas River west to the mountains, locate the source of the Red River, and in turn follow it back east, roughly defining the southern boundary of the new territory.

Pike's detachment moved up the arid plains of the Arkansas Valley and on the afternoon of November 15, 1806, the earnest explorer recorded in his journal that from a small hill he could distinguish a mountain far off to his right, "which appeared like a small blue cloud." More mountains came into view, but this one peak to the north of the river continued to appear to be the highest.

After constructing a breastwork of logs at the present site of Pueblo, where Fountain Creek flows south into the Arkansas, Pike and three companions set out to climb this high peak. Neither the first nor the last to be misled by the scale of Colorado's mountains, Pike thought that the climb would be a day's undertaking. The foursome left the Pueblo stockade at one o'clock on the afternoon of November 25 with the idea of arriving at the mountain's base that evening. Instead, Pike wrote, they found themselves "obliged to take up our night's lodging under a single cedar, which we found on the prairie." The next morning, Pike recorded that he "marched early with an expectation of ascending the mountain, but was only able to encamp at its base, after passing over many small hills covered with cedars and pitch pines."

By the second morning, the explorers' expectations were still not diminished and they "left all of our blankets and provisions at the foot of the mountain, expecting to return to our camp that evening." Alas, that was not to be, and the four endured a frigid bivouac in a small cave without blankets, food, or water. They arose the third morning, Pike reported, "hungry, dry, and extremely sore, from the inequality of the rocks, on which we had lain all night, but amply compensated" for their efforts by views of a sweeping sea of clouds covering the plains below. Surely, this day would see them on the summit.

Within an hour, they reached a summit, all right, but it was only the top of one of the ubiquitous foothills. Pike wrote, the "summit of the Grand Peak, which was entirely bare of vegetation and covered with snow, now appeared at the distance of 15 or 16 miles from us, and as high again as what we had ascended." Pike concluded that it would have taken yet another day—or more—to reach its base. By then, without food or adequate gear, Pike conceded "no human being could have ascended to its pinnacle" in the existing winter conditions. It was November 27, 1806, and the first recorded expedition to attempt to climb a Colorado fourteener turned around and descended to its main camp on the Arkansas River.

Zebulon Montgomery Pike proceeded to entangle himself in the labyrinth of Colorado's geography and the intrigue of Spanish politics, but Pikes Peak remains his greatest claim to fame. In the years ahead, hundreds, thousands, and then hundreds of thousands would follow his footsteps up Colorado's fourteen-thousand-foot peaks.

Pikes Peak rises above a sea of clouds

Sunset shadows on Mount Evans, Mount Bierstadt and the Sawtooth.

Introduction —
Climbing Colorado's Highest Mountains

After Zebulon Pike turned back from his attempt to climb Pikes Peak, it fell to Edwin James, a botanist with Major Stephen Long's 1820 exploration of the Great Plains, to lead the first documented ascent of a Colorado fourteener. As the Long expedition moved up the South Platte River, the mountain that would eventually be named for its leader appeared to the west. At first, Long and James thought this might be Pike's great mountain, but as the explorers moved south along the Front Range, another peak loomed beyond the Platte–Arkansas divide. Convinced that this was indeed Pike's "Grand Peak," twenty-three-year-old James and two companions determined to reach its summit.

The trio passed mineral springs that would later be called "Manitou" and started up the mountain, camping the first evening below timberline. The next morning, July 14, 1820, they climbed into the alpine tundra and botanist James delighted in collecting numerous plants and wildflowers. Later that afternoon, James and his two companions reached the summit of the great peak.

Native Americans, including Arapaho on Longs Peak, Spanish explorers, and French trappers may have reached the summit of this or other fourteeners earlier, but this was the first documented ascent of a Colorado fourteener. After a high altitude bivouac, James and his party descended to their base camp only to find that their smoldering campfire had set fire to several acres of surrounding forest and earned them another distinction—Colorado's first careless campers!

By 1858, Pikes Peak had a crude trail to its summit and suffragette and mountaineer Julia A. Holmes became the first woman to reach the top of a Colorado fourteener. Gold was discovered along Cherry Creek and the South Platte River that same year and soon a rush of "Fifty-niners" with signs of "Pikes Peak or Bust" painted on their wagons poured across the Great Plains. For a time, the Front Range dammed this flood of humanity. But the lure of bigger bonanzas in the mountains to the west soon caused the tidal wave to flow up rocky valleys and spill across high mountain passes into the inner

Mount Elbert, Colorado's highest peak

Rockies, inexorably entwining the stories of Colorado's mountains and its people.

A decade later, Colorado was a territory fighting for statehood and the principal mountaineering goal had become Longs Peak. Reports that the mountain was unclimbable only fueled interest in a first ascent. Finally, on August 23, 1868, after a long approach from Grand Lake, a party that included explorer John Wesley Powell and newspaperman William N. Byers followed young L.W. Keplinger to the summit up what is still called Keplinger's Couloir. A month later, Powell made the first ascent of Mount Powell in the Gore Range and then set about preparing for his famous descent of the Colorado River.

Powell's later surveys of the West coincided with those of Ferdinand Vandemeer Hayden and Lieutenant George Wheeler. Working for the Department of the Interior and the War Department, respectively, the Hayden and Wheeler surveys crisscrossed Colorado's mountains during the 1870s and made numerous first ascents. Those 14,000-foot summits that the surveyors avoided—including most of the Elks, the Crestones, and Wetterhorn—were frequently deemed both "inaccessible" and, conveniently, "unnecessary for topographical purposes."

A generation or two later, a cadre of adventurers finished what the surveys had begun by focusing on mountaineering, rather than topographic, purposes and being challenged rather than deterred by claims of inaccessibility. Chief among these were William Cooper, Percy Hagerman and Harold Clark, Dwight Lavender and the San Juan Mountaineers, and Albert Ellingwood.

Beginning when he was twenty-two, William Cooper covered a wide range of territory in the Needles and the Grenadiers, including 1908 first ascents of Pigeon, Vestal, and Arrow with John Hubbard. When a mis-diagnosis of heart problems after that summer prematurely ended his climbing career, Cooper went on to become an eminent botanist and the father of Alaska's Glacier Bay National Monument.

Mount Bierstadt and mountain goat silhouette

During the summers of 1908, 1909, and 1910, Percy Hagerman and Harold Clark teamed together to climb almost every major summit in the Elks. Their climbing legacy became *Notes on Mountaineering in the Elk Mountains*. Dwight Lavender's legacy was *The San Juan Mountaineers' Climbing Guide to Southwestern Colorado*, which recounted routes pioneered throughout the San Juans during the early 1930s by Lavender and his circle of climbing cohorts, notably T. M. "Mel" Griffiths and Carleton Long.

Albert Ellingwood was perhaps Colorado's preeminent technical climbing pioneer. Born in Iowa, Ellingwood became a Rhodes scholar, professor of political science, and university administrator at Northwestern, but he reserved his deepest passion for the mountains of Colorado and Wyoming. Among his first ascents were the Crestones, Lizard Head, Ellingwood Ridge on La Plata Peak, Ellingwood Arete on Crestone Needle, the Middle and South Tetons, Turret, Warren, Helen, and Sacajawea peaks in the Wind Rivers, and

only the third ascent of the Grand Teton.

Ah, those were the days!

Out of those early days with Ellingwood came two more Colorado climbing legends: the grand man of Colorado's mountains, Carl Blaurock, and the dean of Colorado guidebook authors, Robert Ormes. Blaurock climbed his first mountain—Pikes Peak—in 1909 at the age of fifteen. Three years later, the Colorado Mountain Club was formed. Carl joined immediately and Bill Ervin soon became his inseparable climbing buddy. Carl was short and wiry; Bill was tall and lean and 10 years his senior. They made a good team.

One day atop Blanca Peak, Carl and Bill started checking off all of their fourteener climbs. When counting showed that they had made quite a dent in the list—then totaling 46 peaks—they vowed to finish it, which they did in 1923, becoming the first to do so. (As new surveys added more fourteeners, the pair dutifully climbed the newcomers.)

Not surprisingly, Albert Ellingwood became

the third person to climb all of Colorado's fourteeners. Mary Cronin became the fourth person and first woman on the list in 1934. Carl Blaurock, by the way, went on to climb all of the fourteeners in the United States, finishing his last four California fourteeners in 1957 at the age of 63.

And then there was Ormes. What Fred Beckey was to the Cascades, Norman Clyde to the Sierras, and Leigh Ortenburger to the Tetons, Robert Ormes was to Colorado's mountains. A long-time English professor at Colorado College, Bob Ormes cut his teeth climbing with Ellingwood in the 1920s and went on to such pioneering technical feats as the first ascent of Chimney Peak and the first traverse of Needle Ridge, both in 1934 with Mel Griffiths.

In the early 1950s, the publications committee of the Colorado Mountain Club—which included Carl Blaurock—asked Ormes to edit a guidebook to Colorado's mountains. First published in 1952 and written from Colorado Mountain Club trip reports and Ormes' own numerous outings, *Guide to the Colorado Mountains* quickly became the centerpiece of Colorado mountaineering literature. Ormes was not always right—an uneasy situation that only a fellow guidebook author can truly understand—but none of us who learned to climb in the 1950s and 1960s went into Colorado's mountains without him. More than fifty years and ten editions later, "Ormes" remains in print.

When I first pondered writing a fourteener guidebook in the early 1970s, few of us could have imagined how much Colorado would change in the next quarter of a century and what a special allure the fourteeners would come to hold. In some respects, it was quite predictable; after all, mountains had influenced Colorado's development since the first gold rush. In other respects, it was quite unthinkable. Climbing twenty of Colorado's fourteeners on weekdays during the summer of 1972, Omar Richardson and I encountered a grand total of four other climbers—not on one peak, but the entire summer!

Sunlight and Windom in storm light

By 1975, Lyndon J. Lampert and I were at work on what became *A Climbing Guide to Colorado's Fourteeners*. Building on history first set down by John L. Jerome Hart in his 1925 *Fourteen Thousand Feet* and later by Bill Bueler in *Roof of the Rockies*, we fed our own interests by chronicling the history of these peaks and writing full-blown route descriptions. The first edition of the guide was published in 1978 and over the next twenty-five years it went through three major editions and fifteen printings before going out-of-print in 2003.

In those twenty-five years, Colorado changed quite a bit. Colorado's mountains changed even more. Colorado's population doubled from 2.2 million in 1970 to 4.3 million in 2000. Visitation to Colorado's fourteeners grew from hundreds annually to an estimated 500,000 in 2003. Where once there were three principal Colorado outdoor guidebooks (Ormes, Borneman and Lampert, and Caryn and Peter Boddie's *Hiker's Guide to Colorado*) there are now hundreds of statewide and local guides. These chronicle everything from county highpoints to individual wilderness areas and include two outstanding fourteener guides by world-class mountaineer Gerry Roach and ski aficionado Lou Dawson.

All of these changes were well under way by 1993, when a meeting was held at the old Colorado Mountain Club offices on West Alameda in Denver to discuss increased use of Colorado's fourteeners and the resulting environmental impacts. Out of this meeting came the formation of the Colorado Fourteeners Initiative, a volunteer-based organization committed to preserving Colorado's fourteeners through resource restoration, minimum-impact trail and route delineations, and public education and stewardship programs. These efforts will not roll back the clock, of course, but they have already gone a long way toward ensuring that we will always be celebrating the newness and freshness of Colorado's highest mountains. If you think that it is possible to separate Colorado from its mountains, turn these pages and think again.

Sunset over Grays and Torreys

Front Range —
Rising from the Plains

Longs
Evans and Bierstadt
Grays and Torreys
Pikes

For those traveling across the plains and reaching Colorado from the east, the Front Range is always the opening scene of Colorado's mountain drama. After all of these years, I still cannot fail to stare. On a clear day, you are in sight of at least one of the giants of Longs Peak, Mount Evans or Pikes Peak anywhere from Wyoming to New Mexico. For a good part of the distance, all three peaks are in view, perhaps no more spectacularly than from Denver International Airport. In fact, no view emphasizes the range's name and its dominance above the plains more so. Jet airliners have replaced covered wagons, but the mountain vistas endure.

MOUNTAIN GOAT ON MOUNT EVANS

In broad terms, the Front Range is the continuous line of mountains that borders the high plains from Wyoming southward to Cañon City and the Arkansas River, a distance of roughly 180 miles. The Continental Divide meanders through the northern part of the range before making a swing westward between the Tenmile and Mosquito ranges. Of Colorado's 54 fourteeners, only Grays and Torreys have summits squarely on the crest of the Divide.

The South Platte River is the dominant drainage on the eastern slope of the Front Range, while the Colorado and Arkansas rivers head on its western slope—the former west, and the latter east, of the Continental Divide. The western boundary of the Front Range is not so clearly defined as its obvious eastern rampart, but it is roughly the broad valleys of North, Middle and South parks.

Geologically, the Front Range is the longest continuous uplift in the state. It is also a textbook case of an anticline range. On most peaks, younger overlaying sedimentary layers have long since eroded away, exposing older, Precambrian granite, gneiss and schist. Some remnants of the tilted and broken sedimentary layers are well displayed, however, in formations at the Garden of the Gods in Colorado Springs and on Boulder's Flatirons. Later igneous intrusions were responsible for most gold and silver deposits, while volcanic activity just west of Pikes Peak made Cripple Creek one of Colorado's greatest gold camps.

As the mining boom spread westward, into Colorado's mountains after 1859, gutsy narrow

Sunrise alpenglow reflects in Chasm Lake, below Longs Peak's dramatic east face. defined by the 1,500-foot wall of The Diamond

gauge railroads battled their way up winding Front Range canyons to capture the traffic of Leadville, the Gunnison country and the San Juans. The Colorado Central built up Clear Creek Canyon west of Denver. The Denver, South Park and Pacific snaked through the South Platte Canyon and crossed Kenosha Pass into South Park. The Denver and Rio Grande swung around Pikes Peak and wrestled control of the Royal Gorge away from the Santa Fe to reach Leadville from the south. But the Front Range was tough. For all of these efforts, there would not be a rail line with interstate connections directly west from Denver until the completion of the Moffat Tunnel and the Dotsero Cutoff in 1934.

It's difficult to say which of Colorado's mountain ranges has undergone the most change in the last 50 years, but the Front Range is a prime candidate. The numbers of us who remember seeing miles upon miles of vacant land between Colorado Springs and Denver, winding up U.S. 6 over Loveland Pass, or traveling the Boulder Turnpike through countryside are dwindling. There are certainly a lot more of us crowded in and along the Front Range these days. But thanks to wilderness designations stemming from the 1964 Wilderness Act, one can still find some measure of solitude. Rocky Mountain National Park, the Indian Peaks (absent a summer weekend) and the newer wilderness areas that have been designated since 1993 come to mind.

Growth aside, the Front Range remains the first impression of "the mountains" of Colorado to many. It remains to all of us who live and visit here to see that our experiences and conduct in those mountains ensure that they will forever remain "the mountains" representative of Colorado's wilderness legacy.

Torreys Peak and Grays Peak
from Glacier Mountain

Two magnificent beacons of the Front Range, Pikes Peak (left) and Mount Evans

Respect for the Contrasts

Longs Peak is a tough mountain. Even by its standard route—the Keyhole–Narrows–Homestretch combination—it is no walk-up. That's all the more reason then to be amazed at the multitude attempting its summit each year. For many—particularly those from flatter regions— Longs Peak is a rite of passage and likely the hardest mountaineering they will ever do. Two a.m. starts with headlamps—usually reserved for Northwest volcanoes—are commonplace on Longs in July and August. Some people take fifteen, eighteen, even twenty hours to make the 16-mile, 4,800-foot vertical climb. But more power to them—as long as they respect the mountain for what it is.

One early June day in 1977, I was the only person on the mountain, and had to chop steps in snow and ice to get across the Narrows. I was also on Longs on a recent Sunday in early August when the biggest challenge was avoiding being pushed off the top of the Trough by a gung-ho flatlander hell-bent on the summit. When I passed him later on the Homestretch, he gasped, "I've been up more than 30 of these fourteeners and I never saw anything this hard." Indeed, Longs separates the race-to-the-summit-in-tennis-shoes crowd from more rounded mountaineers and always reminds me—no matter how many times I stand on its summit—that, like all mountains, it is a mountain of contrasts and a mountain to be respected.

Lichen-spattered granite
adorns Chasm View,
a dramatic close-up view
of The Diamond

20

The Keyhole

The Trough

The Homestretch leads to Longs Peak's expansive summit plateau

The view from the summit of Mount Evans at sunrise. . .

. . .and sunset

— Mount Bierstadt's Willows —

Those who hiked up Mount Bierstadt from Guanella Pass in by-gone days have fond memories of a classic Colorado climbing obstacle the much-maligned Bierstadt willows. Once there were only rumors of a trail through the three- to five-foot-high vegetation between the road and the base of the peak. Small children and climbers under 5'10" often roped up here. Early morning dew was certain to splash cold and chill one's bare legs. In 2001, the Colorado Fourteeners Initiative completed a defined trail and sections of boardwalk through the willows to reduce visitor impacts and ensure the survival of vital wetlands at the head of Scott Gomer Creek. Newcomers now cruise along the trail with scarcely a thought. The rest of us savor our memories.

"An Easy Day for a Lady"

Prospector Dick Irwin was a promoter to rival any present-day Chamber of Commerce. In 1865, along with John Baker and Fletcher Kelso, Irwin located the Baker Mine on Kelso Mountain in the shadow of Irwin's Peak. The peak was later renamed for botanist John Torrey, but not before Irwin and his cronies had built a horse trail up neighboring Grays Peak and were charging Colorado's early tourists to ride to the summit and take in the view. The ascents were described as "an easy day for a lady," providing, of course, that she rode horseback to the summit, as most did. Among those to reach the summit of Grays Peak in those days was well-known lecturer, actress, and suffragette, Anna Dickinson. "Never climb without a lemon," was Miss Dickinson's advice to would-be mountaineers.

Overlooking Stevens Gulch to Grays and Torreys peaks

Storm clouds swirl over the Chicago Lakes basin, then. . .

A Painter of the West

Long before color photography books, the way to move a crowd to "oohs" and "ahs" was to display a painting of grand sights known only to a few. No painter did more to promote Colorado's mountains in the 1860s and 1870s than Albert Bierstadt, perhaps the best-known Western landscape painter of his generation. Beginning with a trip to Wyoming's South Pass in 1858, Bierstadt captured the fresh beauty of the West's natural wonders. In 1863, while en route to Yosemite, Bierstadt and Fitz-Hugh Ludlow, a writer for the Atlantic Monthly, camped at Chicago Lakes north of Mount Evans. They called the mountain "Rosalie," Ludlow wrote, after "a dear absent friend of mine and Bierstadt's." The much-admired Rosalie Osbourne later married Ludlow, but after his death, she accepted Bierstadt's proposal as well. Bierstadt's "Storm in the Rocky Mountains" shows the fury of the summer weather above the Chicago Creek campsite on that 1863 trip.

Pikes Peak's north face in winter

Longs Peak is the highest point in Rocky Mountain National Park

MOSQUITO RANGE & TENMILE RANGE — MINING MONARCHS

Lincoln, Bross and Democrat
Sherman
Quandary

One of my wife's favorite photographs shows the two of us in the very early days of our courtship atop Mount Democrat. Long used to climbing with a bunch of guys, Marlene has a big smile on her face and an arm draped nonchalantly around my neck. I am staring stoically straight ahead and standing rigidly with my hands clasped in front of me. But if you take a closer look, there is—I say, at least—the faintest hint of a smile on my face for possibilities to come.

So, take a closer look at the Mosquito and Tenmile ranges. At first blush, these peaks have the reputation of flat summits and easy walk-ups, but that hardly begins to give them their due. With safe snow conditions and proper experience, Quandary Peak's broad south couloir is a ski or glissade "must." The amphitheater at the head of Platte Gulch on the north side of Democrat is a truly awesome place.

BRISTLECONE PINES ON MOUNT BROSS

And Mount Sherman—even without all of its mining history—has one of the best views in the state. Can you count all of the visible fourteeners?

What about their high neighbors? Fourteen of the one hundred highest ranked summits in Colorado rise within the confines of five 7.5-minute quads in the Mosquito and Tenmile ranges. Besides the five official fourteeners, there are Fletcher Mountain (13,951), Pacific Peak (13,950), Crystal Peak (13,852), and "Atlantic Peak" (unnamed 13,841) in the Tenmile Range, and Horseshoe Mountain (13,898), Mount Buckskin (13,865), Clinton Peak (13, 857), Dyer Mountain (13,855), and Mount Silverheels (13,822) in the Mosquitos. Add to these unranked (because of shoulder drops less than 300 feet) Gemini Peak (13,951), "Drift Peak" (unnamed 13,900), and Traver Peak (13,852), and this is indeed a lofty place.

The uncharacteristic ruggedness of
Mount Democrat's west face

And don't forget Mount Cameron! At 14,238 feet, this centerpiece of the Lincoln–Democrat–Bross triangle has been much-maligned but almost always visited in the course of the L–D–B circuit. Indeed, as fellow guidebook author Gerry Roach has aptly pointed out, fifty more feet and Cameron would be the celebrated monarch of the range. Of course, you may also want to wander across Bross's flat summit to the 14,020-foot contour of "South Bross" just in case Gerry ever checks your list.

Although both ranges are rich in mining history and almost always lumped together because of their proximity, there are differences between the Tenmile and Mosquitos. Perhaps most striking is that the Continental Divide runs west from Hoosier Pass along North Star Mountain and divides the two. The Tenmile Range is on the western slope at the headwaters of the Colorado's Blue River tributary, and the Mosquito peaks are on the eastern slope at the headwaters of the South Platte and Arkansas rivers.

Geologically, the Tenmile Range is a continuation of the faulted anticline structure of the Gore Range and is split from it only by the narrow, glacially-carved canyon of Tenmile Creek—the route of I-70 south of Frisco. The Mosquitos are part of the faulted anticline system of the Sawatch Range. Both ranges offer strong evidence of glaciation, such as the cirque below Horseshoe Mountain south of Mount Sherman and the north face of Quandary. So, don't overlook the possibilities—and always kiss your sweetheart in those summit photos.

A winter view of Mount Bross & Mount Lincoln from south of Hoosier Pass

Mount Sherman's Mining Legacy

Long a traditional "first fourteener" because of its rolling slopes and short elevation gain, Mount Sherman nestles inconspicuously north of the easily recognized cirque of Horseshoe Mountain. Sherman's greatest claim to fame, however, lies with two once-roaring boom towns and one great mine that lay at its base. Horseshoe, incorporated in 1881, once boasted a post office, two stores, two hotels, a smelter, a sawmill, and a population of 300.

The real metropolis of the valley, however, was Leavick. Named for Felix Leavick, an early prospector, the town depended on the revenues of the Hilltop Mine, located on the southern slopes of Mount Sherman. A two-and-one-half-mile aerial tramway carried buckets of silver ore, four hundred pounds per bucket, from the mine shaft to a mill in Leavick. The silver crash of 1893 brought Hilltop operations to a halt almost overnight, but mine owners soon discovered the mine's potential for yielding high-grade zinc ore. Zinc production reached such levels by 1896 that the Denver, South Park and Hilltop Railroad was incorporated to extend a ten-mile spur to Leavick. Much of the grade is still visible today.

Mount Sherman and remnants of the Hilltop Mine

Quandary Peak reflection in McCullough Gulch

Mount Lincoln and Quandary Peak from the broad summit of Mount Bross

Rumors of 17,000-foot Giants

As Colorado's first mining boom spilled westward up its many valleys, some prospectors were attracted to placer gold in the western reaches of South Park. The headquarters town of Fairplay was established there in 1859. As the rush spread into the higher mountains west of town, Judge Wilbur F. Stone pondered a name for his new mining company. He left that line blank in the incorporation papers until a passing mosquito obliged by landing directly in the empty space. Judge Stone smashed the pesky critter and took inspiration from the resulting smear to incorporate the Mosquito Mining Company. Later, the name was adopted for the entire mountain range. Stone's subsequent climb of Mount Lincoln and his assertion that the peak was well over 17,000 feet inspired a host of other climbs. Not until 1869 did Josiah Whitney lead the first class of Harvard's School of Mining—a grand total of four young men—to Colorado and through ascents both in the Mosquitos and what came to be called the Collegiate Peaks put to rest rumors of 17,000-foot giants.

Mount Lincoln's north slopes reflecting in an icy tarn above Platte Gulch

A mirror image of Mount Democrat in Kite Lake,
a familiar site to those destined to attempt the
single-day Democrat–Lincoln–Bross trifecta

Quandary Peak's graceful east slopes

After ascending Mount Sherman's south ridge (top),
the summit offers endless views of the Sawatch Range to the west

Mount Sherman's long summit ridge, as viewed from Iowa Gulch

Sawatch Range —
Crest of the Continent

Holy Cross
Massive, Elbert and La Plata
Oxford, Belford, Missouri and Huron
Harvard, Yale, Columbia and Princeton
Antero, Shavano and Tabeguache

In early June of 1967, fresh from ninth grade, six of us Cañon City lads set off to climb Mount Yale. It was twice as high as the 7,000-footers we had been practicing on near our hometown, but no matter. After a camp west of Buena Vista, we headed up Denny Creek—neither the first nor the last to confuse it with Denny Gulch. Denny Creek swung west and so did we.

Up ahead, a mountain towered above snowy slopes. Never mind that one of our number pointed back east to a much higher summit and averred that the summer before with his Boy Scout troop "that had been Mount Yale." Nah, the rest of us chided him. We knew where Mount Yale was and it was right up ahead. So, westward we went until we stood atop our "Mount Yale." It wasn't, of course, but it hardly mattered. The world fell away from my feet that June day and the view of peak after peak of snow-covered

A PATRIOTIC TRIBUTE ON MOUNT ELBERT

ridges convinced me that this was a place where I would spend as much time as I could.

With fifteen fourteeners, this central core of Colorado is indeed the crest of the North American continent. After the Continental Divide swings west around the headwaters of the Arkansas River, it runs almost due south between the massive mountains of the Sawatch and the rugged spires of the Elks. Like a row of stone mammoths, peak after peak lines up to confront the Arkansas Valley.

Geologically, the Sawatch is a huge faulted anticline—older sedimentary layers lifted as a block. More recent igneous intrusions introduced minerals, although the richest deposits of gold and silver occur on the fringes of the range. One major intrusion, the Princeton Batholith, is the source of both Mount Princeton's Chalk Cliffs and the gem field on Mount Antero.

Mount Yale and its prominent southeastern sub-peak dominate the view north from the Ptarmigan Creek basin

After Professor Josiah Whitney's early work in the Collegiate Peaks, the Hayden Survey covered the Sawatch fairly thoroughly. On its heels came the miners and Leadville quickly became the silver siren. Wagon roads and then railroads clawed their way to the "Cloud City" and quickly looked westward across the range. Independence, Cottonwood, Tincup, and Marshall passes were likely routes. William Jackson Palmer's Denver and Rio Grande Railway and John Evans's Denver, South Park, and Pacific raced to build across the Sawatch Range for both the mineral wealth of the Gunnison country and the ripening plum of a transcontinental route to the west. The Rio Grande purchased an Otto Mears toll road across Marshall Pass and won the race only because the South Park chose the Chalk Creek Valley between Princeton and Antero and paused to build the epic Alpine Tunnel. The only standard-gauge

railroad to cross the Sawatch was the Colorado Midland, boring the Hagerman Tunnel under the Continental Divide north of Mount Massive in 1887 while en route to Aspen.

What booms the Sawatch saw in the twentieth century focused on water—the white gold of winter snows covering ski runs and the liquid gold of water flowing eastward through trans-mountain diversion projects to water Front Range growth. Meanwhile, the excitement of one-weekend-a-summer kayak races on the Arkansas River downstream from Salida has grown into a mega-rafting industry up and down the river. All of this has meant more people throughout the area. Today, there is no mistaking Mount Yale—just follow the crowds.

Oxford, Belford and Missouri Mountain from the east ridge of Quail Mountain

A mid-July snowstorm coats Missouri Mountain with a hint of winter, Missouri Basin
FACING PAGE: La Plata Peak looms over the North Fork Clear Creek valley

"Massive" Mount Oklahoma

Carl Blaurock and Bob Ormes aside, the title of "Mr. Fourteener" belongs to retired Denver attorney Jim Gehres. By 2001, Jim's feet had taken him to the summit of each of Colorado's fifty-four fourteeners a dozen times—648 ascents. But even for this Colorado climbing legend, it was not always easy. In 1963, early in his climbing career, Jim set off up North Halfmoon Creek for his first climb of Mount Massive. Arriving on what he thought was the summit, he was amused to find a jar containing a note reading "Mount Oklahoma." It was obviously the

work, Jim thought, of some overly ambitious Sooner. Ignoring the notation and blissfully oblivious to the massive hulk of another mountain rising across the basin to the east, Jim descended, but not back into the North Halfmoon Creek valley toward Leadville. Somehow, he mistakenly headed west into the Fryingpan drainage only to be found by his worried wife many hours later on the road to Aspen. He had indeed climbed 13,845-foot Mount Oklahoma and the real Mount Massive would have to wait for another day.

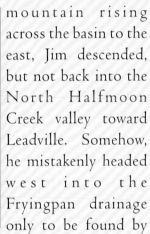

Mount Massive reigns over Native Lake
in the Mount Massive Wilderness

Storm clouds gather around the summit of Mount of the Holy Cross
FACING PAGE: Holy Cross's namesake snow couloir is best seen from nearby Notch Mountain

Mount Princeton's Chalk Cliffs

Seen from the upper Arkansas Valley or the slopes of Trout Creek Pass, Mount Princeton presents three distinct summits, the lower two flanking the higher central peak in near-perfect symmetry. On its southern slopes, however, Princeton drops off abruptly in an escarpment known as the Chalk Cliffs. At least one legend asserts that the cliffs are the hiding place of treasure secreted there centuries ago by Spanish raiders from New Mexico. In reality, the cliffs are not chalk, but crumbling, white quartz monzonite.

The symmetry of Mount Princeton's trio of summits

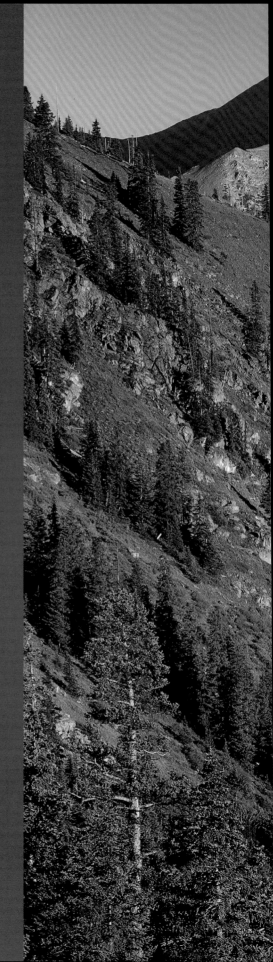

ABOVE: A perfect summer morning reflection of Mount Massive
RIGHT: An uncommon view of Mount Elbert from the southeast,
with Mount Massive rising beyond

Looking up the Three Elk Creek valley to Mount Columbia
FACING PAGE: The beauty of a Colorado sunset unfolds in the skies over La Plata Peak

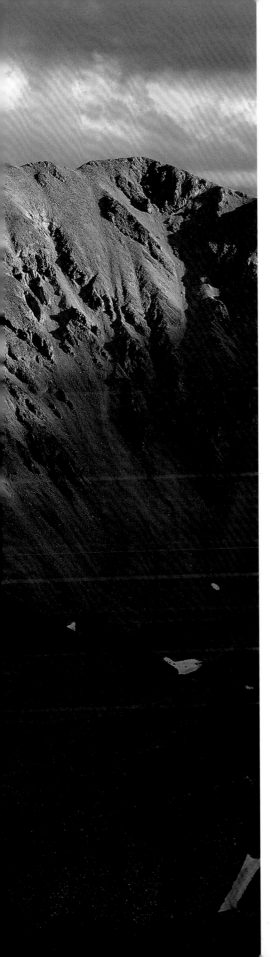

The lure of Colorado's fourteeners reaches far beyond
the state's borders, as the above license plate affirms.
The vehicle belonged to a gem-hunter looking for
aquamarine on the slopes of Mount Antero (top)
LEFT: Mount Shavano and Tabeguache Peak present
an impressive profile across the Browns Creek
drainage south of Mount Antero

63

The striking gold of autumn mixes with sage and pine below Mount Oxford
FACING PAGE: Mount Antero reflects in a tarn in Baldwin Gulch

La Plata's Ridges

On July 26, 1873, pioneer Denver newspaperman William N. Byers of the *Rocky Mountain News* followed James Gardner of the Hayden Survey to the summit of La Plata Peak—"silver" in Spanish. Ascending the long northwest ridge, Byers noted the abundance of raspberries, strawberries, and sky-blue forget-me-nots. "The world seems made of mountains," Byers reported from on top, "a chaotic mass of rocky ridges, peaks and spurs." The most incredible of these is La Plata's two-mile-long northeast ridge. In 1921, the daring Albert Ellingwood made the first ascent of the ridge and returned to camp that evening gleefully reporting that he had dangled from a finger ledge for a full two minutes.

ABOVE: From the summit of La Plata Peak, the craggy contours of Ellingwood Ridge precede a view northeast to Mount Elbert
FACING PAGE: Mount Yale rises majestically above Taylor Park, as seen from the summit of American Flag Mountain

Frenchman Creek provides a less-traveled route up Mount Columbia

FACING PAGE: Much of the east slopes trail to Mount Princeton's summit can be seen from 12,000 feet

Mount Harvard and the upper portion of Horn Fork Basin from the summit of Mount Columbia
FACING PAGE: Lake Ann plays host to a reflection of Huron Peak in the Collegiate Peaks Wilderness

A blush of alpenglow paints Mount Elbert (left) and Mount Massive at sunrise,
while the upper Arkansas River Valley lies hidden below the fog

The Angel of Shavano

Mount Shavano and Tabeguache Mountain are two of only four Colorado fourteeners to bear names of Native American origin. Shavano was a prominent chief of the Tabeguache branch of the Utes. (Antero was a chief of the Uintah Utes and Uncompahgre is a Ute word said to mean "hot water spring.") After Holy Cross's snowy marking and Snowmass's namesake snowfield, the most easily recognized snow feature in Colorado is that which forms in years of adequate snow in the bowl on the southeast side of Mount Shavano. With a head, body, and outstretched wings, the Angel of Shavano has given rise to a host of legends.

One particular legend says that long ago as severe drought gripped the area, a Ute princess knelt at the foot of Mount Shavano and prayed for rain. The god to whom she prayed demanded that she sacrifice herself for the sake of her people. She did so, of course, and every year thereafter, she has reappeared as the Angel of Shavano. The angel weeps for her people, and her tears, symbolic of her sacrifice, provide life-giving moisture to the land below. In the spring of 2002, another drought was so bad that the angel did not appear. Climbing Shavano early that May, my wife, Marlene, and I chanced upon a mountain goat stumbling along a dry streambed looking haggard and badly in need of a drink. We wished him well and spoke of the angel. The next morning there was a foot of new snow on the peaks.

An afternoon of steady rain begins to subside, allowing Mount Harvard to appear
FACING PAGE: Tabeguache Peak and Mount Shavano from the south

Photographer on Wilson Peak, 1931

Fourteeners in Time

Clearing storm, Crestone Peaks & Kit Carson Mountain, 1920

Photographs from the
Archives of the
Colorado Mountain Club

Wetterhorn Peak, 1929

Mount of the Holy Cross, 1921

The Narrows, Longs Peak, 1913

The Narrows, Longs Peak, 1913

Climbers on ledges, Maroon Peak, 1933

Snowstorm on Redcloud Peak, 1929

North Eolus Peak & Twin Thumbs Pass, 1937

Grays & Torreys Peaks, 1915

The view of Mount Eolus from Sunlight Peak, 1920

A cloudy day at camp, Chicago Basin, 1920

The Crestone Needle - Crestone Peak traverse, 1920

Blue Lakes from Mount Sneffels, 1920

Swirling clouds & Sunlight Peak summit, 1920

Ascending the Trough, Longs Peak, 1913

Negotiating ledges on Maroon Peak, 1933

Traversing the Catwalk, Mount Eolus, 1927

Wilson Peak from Sunshine Mountain, 1931

On Wilson Peak, with Lizard Head in the distance 1931

The trail up Windom Peak, 1920

Cliff-climbing on Wetterhorn Peak, 1929

Above the clouds on Pikes Peak, date unknown

Mount Wilson & Gladstone Peak, 1931

Wilson Peak from El Diente, 1931

Pyramid Peak & the Maroon Bells from Snowmass Mountain, 1933

El Diente Peak's west ridge, 1931

The Maroon Peaks from Pyramid Peak, 1921

Longs Peak summit silhouettes, 1913

Campfire at Snowmass Lake, 1933

Sangre de Cristo Range — Sentinels of a Spanish Legacy

Crestone Peak, Crestone Needle, Kit Carson and Humboldt
Blanca, Ellingwood, Little Bear and Lindsey
Culebra

Over Christmas vacation in 1971, Omar Richardson and I slept in the drafty shell of his dad's old pick-up and early the next morning skied up the road toward South Colony Lakes. Were we after the Crestones? Of course. We were far too young and inexperienced not to be. Three hours of breaking trail brought us within sight of, well, it must be Crestone Peak! An hour later brought us to our youthful senses. The craggy summit towering ahead was Broken Hand Peak. Crestone Needle and Crestone Peak lay hidden in clouds much farther up the valley. Cold enough for one day, we turned around and skied out.

SOUTH COLONY CREEK RAINBOW

That says a lot about the Sangres—so close, yet so far. The range is uncannily straight and its summits appear deceivingly close when viewed from the adjacent expanses of the San Luis and Wet Mountain valleys. But the highest peaks rise almost 7,000 feet above the valleys and an absence of major foothills makes its numerous canyons generally rocky, deep, and steep. The range is a fault block structure that differs from anticline ranges in that it was lifted as a block with a complete break in the overlaying layers along at least one side, rather than being arched and folded. North of Hayden Pass, the overlaying, older layers have eroded away on the crest of the range, but they are plainly visible on the upper reaches of the southern peaks, particularly in the plentiful nubs of the sedimentary layer of Crestone Conglomerate on Crestone Needle.

After major glaciers sculpted features such as the towering north face of Blanca and its sweeping ridges, Colorado became semi-arid. Once-lush vegetation in the San Luis Valley became sparse. The result was that winds blowing across the valley floor picked up large quantities of topsoil and sand and funneled them toward Mosca and Music passes just south of the Crestones. As the winds rose to cross the range, they dropped their heavy earthly cargo along the western side. These deposits accumulated to heights of seven hundred feet and formed the Great Sand Dunes, one of the most distinctive features of the Sangre de Cristos.

While other Colorado mountain ranges have

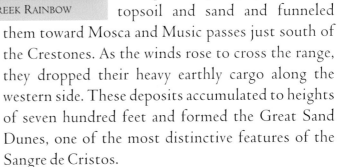

Kit Carson Mountain and the Crestone Peaks mimic 700-foot-high
sand dunes at Great Sand Dunes National Park & Preserve

histories intimately tied to the Anglo mining rushes of the latter 1800s, the Sangre de Cristo Range is more closely tied to Colorado's Hispanic heritage. Its very name is Spanish and means "Blood of Christ." The most common explanation for the name is that an unknown explorer or missionary viewed the colors of a deep red sunset on its peaks from the San Luis Valley and uttered the phrase in a moment of wonder.

In 1820, Mexico declared independence from Spain and the new government quickly granted large parcels of land along its northern frontier to encourage settlement. Six of these grants were wholly or partially in what is now Colorado and two encompassed sizeable portions of the Sangre de Cristos. The Vigil and St. Vrain Grant covered the southern half of the Blanca massif and the eastern slope of the Culebra Range. The Sangre de Cristo Grant bordered the Culebra Range on the west and covered much of the southeastern San Luis Valley, including the site of Colorado's oldest town, San Luis, which was founded in 1851. Conflicts between these Hispanic land grants and subsequent Anglo claims continue to this day and are evidenced most by ownership disputes surrounding Culebra Peak.

The best thing to happen in the Sangre de Cristos recently was the passage of the Colorado Wilderness Bill of 1993. It created the Sangre de Cristo Wilderness Area, a 226,455-acre preserve running almost the entire length of the range from south of Salida to the Great Sand Dunes. Access issues, including those along the infamous Como Lake jeep road, prevented expansion of the wilderness designation southward to include the Blanca massif. Access issues also exempted the heavily traveled road into South Colony Lakes from this legislation, but overall, if each of us does his or her part, this wilderness designation will go a long way toward preserving the sanctity of this special range.

Mount Lindsey from high above Lily Lake; the Spanish Peaks rise in the distance
PREVIOUS PAGES: Sunset rays filter through high peaks of the Sierra Blanca massif

Willow Creek flows below Kit Carson Peak and Challenger Point,
their summits hidden in the clouds

Crestone Needle and Crestone Peak and their dramatic connecting ridge

Looking up Humboldt Peak's northwest shoulder

Blanca Peak's Dominance

Colorado's fourth highest summit dominates the lower San Luis Valley and its circle of neighboring summits in such a striking hierarchy of form that Franklin Rhoda of the Hayden Survey was moved to write in 1875, "Such a beautiful subordination of parts we had not before seen anywhere among the mountains of Colorado."

The one exception to this symmetry is the imposing mile-wide, 1,500-foot high north face of Blanca and Ellingwood peaks rising above Lily Lake and the headwaters of the Huerfano River. Robert Ormes and Harold Wilm made the first ascent of this face near the Blanca–Ellingwood saddle in 1927, while a Colorado College group completed a more direct line straight up to Blanca's summit in 1948.

Blanca Peak's imposing north wall

An alpenglow sunrise illuminates Humboldt Peak, the Crestone peaks, Colony Baldy
and Kit Carson Mountain while fog filters through the Wet Mountain Valley

The setting sun briefly shines on Mount Lindsey's summit

Little Bear, 1943

Little Bear Peak has always been considered one of Colorado's most challenging fourteeners and one devoid of an easy route to the top. Charles Fay and J. R. Edmands made its first ascent by mistake in 1888 while trying to climb Blanca. Once atop Little Bear, one look at the jagged connecting ridge to Blanca convinced them that they had come to the end of their climb. This first climb of Little Bear and the few that followed were made from the south. On a grand day in August 1943, however, Carl Blaurock, Roy Murchison, and Herb Hollister decided to explore Little Bear's west ridge from Como Lake.

"We were in trouble almost immediately," Hollister wrote. "The ridge turned out to be sharp, shattered and rotten. In fact it had plenty of everything wrong with it that any ridge could have. At this point the heavy fog, which obscured the view, was the only thing which prevented me from calling in the dogs and going home. However, by this time I was on the rope between Roy and Carl and since it was tweedle-dee and tweedle-dum whether we moved up or down the ridge, we took a few gulps of the fog and inched on higher."

Forced to move off the main ridge, the trio worked their way along a series of smaller ridges "until there was nothing on which to ascend. This method ultimately brought us out on top," Hollister recalled, "and it was mighty gratifying to learn from the register that we had actually climbed the right mountain."

Little Bear Peak from Ellingwood Point

Ellingwood Point and Blanca Peak are connected to
Little Bear Peak by one of Colorado's toughest ridges

A short respite from the climb allows for
views of Culebra Peak's final push to the summit

Clearing weather reveals the pyramidal shape of Mount Lindsey

The Last to be Climbed

In the summer of 1916, Crestone Peak, Crestone Needle, and Kit Carson Peak were the only unclimbed 14,000-foot mountains in Colorado. They were prizes to be had when Albert Ellingwood and seven others made camp in the high basin of Willow Creek in high spirits that were, in Ellingwood's words, "fed by tales of peaks unclimbed and peaks unclimbable." With relative ease, the party climbed the northwest ridge of Kit Carson—scrambling over its 14,081-foot northwest sub-peak now known as Challenger Point in the process—and made the first documented ascent of Kit Carson. "The more energetic of the party" then moved their camp south to the Spanish Creek drainage to test "the unclimbability of the Crestones."

On July 24, Ellingwood, Eleanor Davis, Frances Rogers, and Joe Deutchbein got an exceptionally late start (8:10 a.m.), but proceeded up Crestone's north arete and into the north couloir,

A panoramic view of Challenger, Kit Carson and the Crestones at sunset

reaching the summit of the main peak shortly before one o'clock. So much for unclimbability! But the Needle beckoned and the party gingerly began to traverse toward it. While later climbers might dispute the ease of Ellingwood's description, he took pleasure in noting that "the gendarmes that stood up like Cleopatra's Needle on the east were of a gentler aspect on the other side, and lent themselves to prudential circumvention."

Halfway across the ridge, Deutchbein and Rogers retreated, but Ellingwood and Davis finished the traverse on the conglomerate-studded northwest wall of Crestone Needle and claimed Colorado's last unclimbed fourteener. Circuitously descending into South Colony Lakes Basin, the pair returned to their campsite via the Crestone Peak-Humboldt saddle, arriving there at 11:15 p.m. There would be no more tales of peaks unclimbed and peaks unclimbable.

Fall color precedes the view of Blanca Peak and Ellingwood Point
in the upper Huerfano River valley
FACING PAGE: Crestone Needle reflects an intense summer sunrise in Lower South Colony Lake

Elk Mountains —
Red, Rugged & Rotten
Castle
Pyramid, Maroon and North Maroon
Capitol and Snowmass

One day in August 1980, I was kicking steps up the southeast couloir on Maroon Peak. The snow was rapidly turning to mush and an ugly thunderhead was building above the reddish ridges. If I had listened to Jim Gehres, I would have been on the standard route to the south and probably close to the summit by now. But there was so much snow—even that late—the narrow slot that guidebook author and skier extraordinaire Lou Dawson would later call the "Garbage Chute" had suckered me in. It was filled with a veritable highway of snow and it looked like it led straight to the top. Far above the chute, I kicked another step and sunk in to my knee. Just ahead, the couloir narrowed considerably and the snow petered out, revealing downsloping cliff bands and a steady stream of loose rock. I did the only thing that I could think of. I turned around.

The Elks are great mountains, but they rarely offer a second chance. With the exception of Castle Peak by its standard route, and maybe Snowmass, the other Elk Range summits almost always make anyone's list of ten toughest Colorado fourteeners. If Cathedral Peak (13,943) north of Castle and "Thunder Pyramid" (unnamed 13,932) south of

MOSS CAMPION DETAIL ON FRIGID AIR PASS

Pyramid were a few feet taller, they would likely make anyone's dozen toughest. In summer, red towers and glistening white thrones tower above rushing streams and meadows ablaze with wildflowers, but these are no walk-ups. In winter—well, most folks are content to look at them from atop Aspen's ski runs.

During the Laramide Orogeny, the sedimentary layers of the reddish Maroon Formation were lifted and tilted to build the Maroon Bells and Castle and Pyramid peaks. About the same time, igneous intrusions formed the white granites of Snowmass Mountain and Capitol Peak. All of these mountains were then subjected to extensive glaciation, the most striking example of which may be the thin, curving aretes high above Pierre Lakes Basin.

Both the Hayden and Wheeler surveys dabbled in the Elks. Hayden topographer Henry Gannett's 1873 climb of the south ridge on Castle Peak involved chimney techniques quite advanced for the time and, in Gannett's words, "afforded more of a climb than any other Colorado mountain with which I have any acquaintance." A Wheeler topographer named Young may have made the first

A summer view of Maroon Bells from Frigid Air Pass,
Maroon Bells-Snowmass Wilderness

ascent of either Pyramid or North Maroon. The record is inconclusive and has been argued both ways.

The silver rush of the late 1870s hit the Elks from both directions. In the southern part of the range and its offshoots, Gothic, Irwin, and Crystal were among those boom towns that rose and fell on the mining wave. To the north, Ute City was founded in 1879 as a silver camp, but went on to other things long after it changed its name to Aspen. Railroads eventually reached Aspen from the north, but the steep passes through the Elks never succumbed to steel rails and remain legendary for their toughness.

In recent years, the Maroon Bells–Snowmass Wilderness Area and those covering the Hunter-Fryingpan drainage and the Raggeds have gone a long way toward preserving the Elks, but—and there always seems to be a qualifier—issues of water, land use, and transportation remain paramount. These are not only mountains but also an entire ecosystem that will not give a second chance.

The dramatic profile of Capitol Peak's
southeast ridge from Silver Creek Pass

Hagerman Peak dominates the view at Snowmass Lake while the
summit of Snowmass Mountain rises in relative insignificance nearby

Turnabout is fair play— Snowmass Lake is but a small, blue orb
far below Snowmass Mountain's vast, east-facing rock glacier

Autumn splendor at the Maroon Bells,
one of Colorado's classic portraits

The Deadly Bells

The big wooden sign with the title "The Deadly Bells" is gone now. It has been replaced by a much smaller bronze plaque. The words are the same, but somehow they don't quite strike the fear that six-inch-high routed letters did, especially on your first visit. We had our picture taken by that sign, heeded its warning, and turned back in an August snowstorm at 12,500 on the North Bell. Over the years, others have not been so lucky. Some fatalities were amateurs in over their heads, but many were accomplished mountaineers caught by icy couloirs, slippery down-sloping strata, and cascading rock fall. Beautiful and majestic, "the Deadly Bells" are among Colorado's toughest fourteeners.

A hiker contemplates tomorrow's climb

Snowmass Mountain reflects in Snowfield Lake
FACING PAGE: Minnehaha Gulch begins to show its autumn color below Pyramid Peak

A predawn glow paints Castle Peak (left) and Cathedral Peak,
the latter just short of Colorado's fourteener ranks, but equally impressive

The interplay of shadow and light on
North Maroon and Maroon peaks, Fravert Basin

Evening light on Pyramid Peak

Capitol's Knife-Edge

The pioneers of mountaineering in the Elks were Percy Hagerman, the son of mining and railroading magnate J. J. Hagerman, and Harold Clark, a prominent Aspen lawyer with substantial mining interests. During the summers of 1908, 1909, and 1910, at the then ripe ages of 39 and 46, respectively, Hagerman and Clark teamed together to climb almost every major summit in the Elks. Their

climbing legacy became *Notes on Mountaineering in the Elk Mountains*, which Hagerman compiled in 1912. Reporting an apparent first ascent of Capitol Peak, Hagerman wrote: "There are no difficulties until the crest of the east ridge is reached two hours from the top. From this point on, the way is on or near the crest of the ridge and the climbing arduous. There is one rather sensational bit of about forty feet where the ridge is so sharp that one must get astride of it and move along on hands and knees. The drop on the north side here is something like 1,500 feet, not straight but appallingly steep and smooth."

Many later climbers would agree with Hagerman's description of Capitol's knife-edge. Hagerman Peak near Snowmass and Clark Peak east of Capitol are named for these mountaineers.

Capitol Peak is most often climbed via its
infamous knife-edge ridge

Alpenglow reflection of Castle Peak,
along the Pearl Pass road

Sunrise on Conundrum Peak (14,022'), Montezuma Basin

Although its elevation places it higher than eight other ranked Colorado fourteeners, Conundrum Peak doesn't make the cut on most bonafide fourteener lists due to its close proximity to neighboring Castle Peak, and a less-than-300-foot vertical drop to the two peaks' connecting saddle. Ironically, nearby North Maroon Peak, and El Diente in the San Miguel Mountains near Telluride, would presumably fail to qualify for these same reasons. Perhaps owing to their inherent difficulty, they still make most recognized lists.

The San Juans —
A Land of Endless Mountains

Uncompahgre and Wetterhorn
Redcloud, Sunshine and Handies
San Luis
Sneffels
Mount Wilson, El Diente and Wilson Peak
Sunlight, Windom and Eolus

Uncompahgre is my favorite fourteener. Given my aversion to "ten best" lists and favorites of any kind, it's difficult to acknowledge that fact, but there is no denying it. Uncompahgre is definitely my favorite fourteener. For years whenever the skies were clear, I watched its rocky profile dominate the southwestern horizon from the windows of Western State College. Uncompahgre was the first fourteener I climbed with best-friend mountain buddies Omar Richardson and Gary Koontz. From Uncompahgre's summit that snowy April day in 1972, the San Juans sprawled endlessly under a pale-blue sky laced with wispy mare's tails and feathery contrails.

SAN JUAN WATERFALL

There was Wetterhorn, close at hand, but looking like a gnarly chocolate chip stuck in a mound of white frosting. Almost in line with Wetterhorn, but miles beyond, Sneffels appeared as a tiny triangle on the range's northern fringe. Sunshine, Redcloud, and Handies rose to the south, but what was that pointed peak even farther south? Rio Grande Pyramid, Gary said. But the real concentration of jagged peaks lay a few degrees to the west. The Needles and Grenadiers looked like an impenetrable maze and still farther west the Wilsons and El Diente rose like a giant fist.

The San Juans are indeed a land of endless mountains. No other range in the contiguous United States boasts as much land above 10,000 feet, and no other Colorado range can equal its ten thousand square miles of rugged peaks, high lakes, narrow valleys, abandoned mines, and preserved wilderness. The Continental Divide enters the heart of this labyrinth well east of Uncompahgre and then makes a great bend to the west deep within the range, making San Juan rivers run toward every point of the compass. The Rio Grande flows east into the San Luis Valley. The Animas, Los Pinos, Piedra, and San Juan flow south toward New Mexico. The Lake Fork of the Gunnison and the Uncompahgre rivers run to the north, and the Dolores and San Miguel drain to the west. Between these drainages, San Juan passes are renowned for being high and often inaccessible.

Geologically, the San Juans are complex. As the Laramide Orogeny pushed up all of Colorado's mountains, a huge mass of molten lava formed a giant blister called the San Juan Dome. Some of the lava made its way to the surface and erupted in extensive volcanic activity. As the volcanic rock cooled, erosive forces that included Quaternary glaciers carved up the landscape. In some areas, water and wind erosion and glaciation were so intense that the volcanic layers were whittled down to

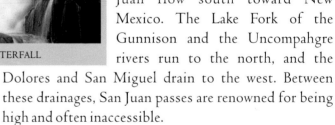

Uncompahgre Peak, the high point of
the vast and mighty San Juan Mountains

expose their Precambrian core, resulting in the sweeping ridges and narrow aretes of the Needles and Grenadiers.

Hayden and Wheeler survey teams climbed many of the highest San Juan summits and mapped the meandering valleys during the early 1870s—just in time for the mining boom that began by decade's end. There were no El Dorado-like bonanzas to be found in the San Juans, but there was gold and silver in enough supply to give birth to scores of mining towns and a few legendary mines. The towns of Sherman, Capitol City, Ouray, Sneffels, Animas Forks, Silverton, Creede, and many more boomed in their turn. Some survive and some are only memories. The Camp Bird mine near Ouray and the Ute-Ulay mine west of Lake City are two of the legends that quickened the pulses of many a would-be tycoon.

Transportation in the San Juans has always been a major challenge. Rocky defiles and high passes—swept in winter by infamous San Juan avalanches—have long resisted all-weather travel. Early miners resorted to skis. Men like Otto Mears first built wagon roads and then narrow gauge railroads to seemingly impossible places. Today, only Lizard Head, Red Mountain, Wolf Creek, Slumgullion/Spring Creek, and North (Cochetopa) passes provide year-round, paved access through the San Juans. During major snowstorms even these may be closed.

In the thirty-some years since my first climb of Uncompahgre, some places in the San Juans seem unchanged, or at least have borne the impacts of change relatively gracefully—Lake City, Silverton, and Ouray come to mind. Other towns have undergone a boom far beyond the wildest dreams of the mining frontier. Durango is much more now than the Silverton train and Telluride—where once I had to look hard to find a meal—mines the white gold of winter snows with a frenzy. In still other locations—Creede for one—the winds of change provoke acrimonious uncertainty.

Someday, I hope to sit on the summit of Uncompahgre with my grandchildren. "So why is this your favorite mountain, Grandpa?" I'll look out across the vastness, probably shed a nostalgic tear or two, and tell them something of skiing up Nellie Creek or Gary teaching me to glissade. I'll point out Wetterhorn, Sneffels, and even Rio Grande Pyramid. Then, I'll suggest that they go and discover their own favorite mountain. The San Juans are filled with possibilities. May it always be so.

Redcloud and Sunshine peaks as viewed from Coney Summit, the high point of the Colorado Trail

Dwight Lavender & the San Juan Mountaineers

The technical climbing history of Mount Sneffels and its imposing neighbors belongs to Dwight Lavender and the San Juan Mountaineers. From 1929 to 1934, Lavender and principal companions Mel Griffiths and Carleton Long made ascents of almost every major peak in the San Juans and chronicled their routes, geology, and history in *The San Juan Mountaineers' Climbing Guide to Southwestern Colorado*. One climb of the east couloir of Sneffels's north face involved some of the most advanced snow and ice climbing done in the state up to that time. Perhaps most amazing, Dwight Lavender accomplished all of this before he died tragically of infantile paralysis at the age of twenty-four.

ABOVE: A panoramic view of the Sneffels Range at sunset
FACING PAGE: Mount Sneffels through the seasons (insets), and from the Blue Lakes Trail

A small tarn at over 12,000 feet reflects Wilson Peak
FACING PAGE: Handies Peak in morning light, Grizzly Gulch
FOLLOWING PAGES: Gladstone Peak (13,913') and Wilson Peak in their winter mantle of snow

Sunrise light on Windom Peak (above) and Sunlight Peak (right),
Sunlight Basin, Weminuche Wilderness

Sunlight Poisoning

Carl Blaurock was quite a character. In his later years—he lived to be almost 99—he regaled me with tales of past climbs in between sips of homemade chokecherry brandy. Not only were Carl and Bill Ervin the first to climb all of Colorado's then recognized fourteeners, but Carl may still be the only one to have stood on his head atop all of them. I asked him why in the world he ever thought of that. Carl threw his head back and chuckled, "Because I wanted to have my feet higher on the mountain than anybody else!" Even on Sunlight? I asked. Of course, Carl had a picture to prove it and a story to boot. "Fella beside me on Sunlight was nervous," Carl said. "Told me afterwards that I could have died of Sunlight poisoning" What did he mean? I asked. Carl grinned. "One drop and it would have killed you."

"Inaccessible" Wetterhorn

William Marshall of the Wheeler Survey climbed Uncompahgre during the summer of 1874, but made no reference to the prior ascent of the Hayden team, an understandable omission given the competition between the two groups. Marshall observed that "the Wetterhorn, to the south of west a few miles from Uncompahgre Peak, is a shark's nose in form, and its ascent being unnecessary for topographical purposes, was not attempted. It exceeds 14,000 in altitude and appears inaccessible."

Wetterhorn Peak and Matterhorn Peak (13,590')
from the slopes of Uncompahgre Peak
ABOVE: Benchmark below Matterhorn Peak   147

Sunset on Sunshine Peak (above) and Handies Peak (right),
two fourteeners that can be viewed near Cinnamon Pass

"Manufactory of Storms"

The Needle Mountains are true to their name. They are rivaled only by the sweeping ridges and jagged summits of the nearby Grenadiers. From the slopes of Uncompahgre in 1874, Franklin Rhoda observed "a group of very scraggy mountains, about which the clouds were continuously circling, as if it was their home." Later from Mount Sneffels, Rhoda remained duly impressed. "We have never yet seen the group from any station (and we have viewed it from all sides)," Rhoda wrote, "without feeling both deep respect and awe for their terrible ruggedness. The fact already stated, that the storm clouds seem to hover about them before starting their meandering way, only served to add to our other feelings one of uneasiness." Neither the Hayden nor Wheeler surveys ventured into the Needles, but Rhoda's assessment that the range was a "manufactory of storms" gave rise to naming its highest peak, "Aeolus," for

the Greek god of the winds. Sunlight and Windom were not named until about 1902 when the area was finally mapped by the U. S. Geological Survey.

LEFT: Storm light on Mount Eolus
ABOVE: The Catwalk leading to Eolus' summit
in more favorable weather

The long, gentle connecting ridge between Redcloud and Sunshine peaks,
as seen from high in Grizzly Gulch

Wetterhorn Peak's pyramidal form, as seen from Wetterhorn Basin

Scared Cats

In the summer of 1921, motivated by "a certain restlessness of feet," Carl Blaurock, Bill Ervin, and Dudley Smith headed to the San Juans to climb fourteeners. Over the course of two weeks, relying only on narrow gauge railroads and an occasional hitched ride, the trio traveled 200 miles on foot, climbed nine fourteeners, and gained 60,000 feet in elevation. Their last summit was Mount Wilson, where, in Carl's words, they scrambled along the peak's summit ridge "like scared cats on a backyard fence."

Two opposing views of the infamous Wilson-El Diente ridge,
featuring Mount Wilson (above, left) and El Diente Peak (above, right)

Mount Wilson, Gladstone Peak and Wilson Peak,
the heart of the San Miguel Mountains,
one of the San Juans' many sub-ranges

Nellie Creek flows below Uncompahgre Peak

Two views of remote San Luis Peak;
a hiker makes his way to the summit via the Stewart Creek approach (top),
and sunset illuminates the peak, as viewed from the Colorado Trail

Mount Eolus and Twin Lakes from Windom Peak
RIGHT: A waterfall along Kilpacker Creek flows below El Diente Peak
PRECEDING PAGES: Shadow and light on Sunlight and Windom peaks

Epilogue — Tomorrow

It is indeed impossible to separate Colorado from its mountains.
There is a part of me that mourns the passing of the way
Colorado's mountains once were. But there is another,
larger part of me that will always be thankful for the way
Colorado's mountains still are. Celebrate them.
Preserve them. May they endure forever.

Sunset from timberline on Culebra Peak,
July, 2004

Bibliography

Prologue
Hart, Stephen Harding, and Archer Butler Hulbert, eds. *Zebulon Pike's Arkansaw Journal: In Search of the Southern Louisiana Purchase Boundary Line*. (Denver: The Stewart Commission of Colorado College and the Denver Public Library, 1932), pp. 118-128. (Pike's account)

Rising from the Plains
Arps, Lousia Ward and Elinor Eppich Kingery. *High Country Names*. (Denver: Colorado Mountain Club, 1966), p. 52. (Dickinson's lemon quote)

Crest of a Continent
Rocky Mountain News, August 3, 1873. (Byers account of La Plata climb)

Red, Rugged and Rotten
Hagerman, Percy. *Notes on Mountaineering in the Elk Mountains of Colorado, 1908-1910*. (Denver: Colorado Mountain Club, 1956), p. 18. (Capitol's knife-edge description)

Sentinels of a Spanish Legacy
Ellingwood, Albert R. "Climbing in the Sangre de Cristo." *Trail and Timberline*. Number 81 (June, 1925), pp. 1-5.
Hollister, Herb. "Little Bear by the West Ridge." *Trail and Timberline*. Number 311 (November, 1944), pp. 127-128.
Annual Report of the United States Geological and Geographical Survey of the Territories, 1875. (Washington: GPO, 1876), p. 306. (Rhoda's Blanca quote)

Land of Endless Mountains
Executive and Descriptive Report of Lieutenant William L. Marshall, Corps of Engineers, on the Operations of Party No. 1, Colorado Section, Field-Season of 1875. (Washington: GPO, 1876), p. 96. (Marshall's 1875 Wetterhorn quote)
Euser, Barbara J. ed. *A Climber's Climber: On the Trail with Carl Blaurock*. (Evergreen, Colorado: Cordillera Press, 1984. (Blaurock quotes)
Annual Report of the United States Geological and Geographical Survey of the Territories, 1874. (Washington: GPO, 1875), pp. 453, 481. (Rhoda's Needles quotes)

And generally...

Borneman, Walter R. and Lyndon J. Lampert. *A Climbing Guide to Colorado's Fourteeners*. (Boulder, Colorado: Pruett Publishing, 1978).

Bueler, William M. *Roof of the Rockies: A History of Mountaineering in Colorado*. (Boulder, Colorado: Pruett Publishing, 1974).

Chronic, John and Halka Chronic. *Prairie, Peak and Plateau: A Guide to the Geology of Colorado*. (Denver: Colorado Geological Survey Bulletin, No. 32, 1972).

Dawson, Louis W. II. *Dawson's Guide to Colorado's Fourteeners*. (Volume 1, The Northern Peaks) (Monument: Blue Clover Press, 1994).

Dawson, Louis W. II. *Dawson's Guide to Colorado's Fourteeners*. (Volume 2, The Southern Peaks) (Monument: Blue Clover Press, 1996).

Eberhart, Perry and Philip Schmuck. *The Fourteeners: Colorado's Great Mountains*. (Chicago: The Swallow Press, 1970).

Hart, John L. J. *Fourteen Thousand Feet: A History of the Naming and Early Ascents of the High Colorado Peaks*. (Denver, Colorado Mountain Club, 1925).

Roach, Gerry. *Colorado's Fourteeners: From Hikes to Climbs*. (Golden: Fulcrum Publishing, 1992).

Index

(Italicized numbers denote pages with photos; entries such as "Mount Elbert" are indexed under "Elbert, Mount.")

About the Photographs

This book has been in the making for many years, but it got a significant boost early in 2004. I got a call from Walt Borneman, asking if I had ever considered doing a coffee table book featuring the fourteeners. Walt and I, along with Lou Dawson and Gerry Roach, had participated in a speaking engagement benefitting the Colorado Fourteeners Initiative (they spoke, I showed photos), and after listening to Walt wax eloquently about Colorado's fourteeners, I knew I wanted him to be a significant part of the project. He had no way of knowing this when he called, but I had actually done some preliminary cover designs that included his name. Two weeks after our initial discussion, I had Walt's brilliant manuscript in my hands. Ah, serendipity!

Over the course of two decades photographing Colorado's incredible landscape, the fourteeners have been a special draw for me. Having lived in Colorado Springs in my formative years, Pikes Peak was a constant and willing photographic subject. From there it was only natural that I expand my image roster to include as many of Colorado's highest peaks as possible. Along the way I've been rewarded time after time with incredible light; enjoyed watching silently as herds of elk grazed nearby, unaware of my presence; been chased off many a mountain by lightning storms I was sure had been preordained to seek me out; and even gotten myself lost while hiking back to the trailhead in the dark, with precious film of the evening's spectacular sunset in my camera. Even though I most often travel alone, I especially cherish the times that I've been able to spend on the trail with friends.

Unlike Walt, I have not climbed all of Colorado's fourteeners. Can't really say whether or not I ever will. The burden 40 pounds of large-format camera gear imposes on the human frame above timberline often dictates where I go. While I've stood on the summits of several, I've always thought that, from a photographic standpoint, the views were always better *of* fourteeners than *from* them. It's not like being among the highest mountains in the state rather than atop them is without its physical challenges. I've hiked, backpacked and bushwhacked among the best of Colorado, and come away with a lifetime's worth of photographic memories. The best part is, I'm not done yet! Being in Colorado's high country is my passion. Come any given summer's day, that's where you'll find me, most likely trudging up the trail in the predawn darkness, hoping for that magic 30 seconds of fleeting first light.

In compiling the images for this book, I concluded that my inventory came up a little short. So I turned to Dave Showalter and David Anschicks, two photographers whose work I had admired for quite some time. While their photos don't rise to any sort of *numerical* advantage, this would have been an incomplete story without their images. Their fresh perspectives have made this a far more compelling document than it otherwise would have been, and I'm grateful for their participation in the project.

As if including photos by two great contemporaries isn't good enough, I was thrilled at the chance to rummage through big, thick photo albums in the archives room of the Colorado Mountain Club and select some classic photos to be included in the book. It was a thrilling and humbling experience to see images dating as far back as 1913, long before so many of today's technological advances made backcountry travel so much safer and more comfortable. Love that waterproof, breathable shell covering your wicking layer? Try wearing heavy wool. Getting good traction from that aggressive tread on your composite boots? Try hammering a few nails into the soles of your boots. Then there's the issue of access. These early adventurers were journeying into places that, unlike today, hadn't yet seen the armies of climbing enthusiasts beating familiar paths to their highest summits. Back then, getting to the trailhead was sometimes as much of an adventure as the actual climb is today! Even so, some early trips in the Colorado high country shortly after the start of the twentieth century were quite the social affair, with mess halls staffed by cooks, heavy canvas tents to ward off a cool wind, and once in a while, a grand theatrical production played out around the flickering light of a campfire. (Makes me wonder why I travel alone most of the time.) I'd like to thank Kristy Judd, executive director of the CMC, for allowing me access to, and usage of, these precious images.

— Todd Caudle

Photographers' Index

All photographs in this book are by Todd Caudle, except:
Dave Showalter: pages 47, 55, 67, 71, 120, 121, 146-147
David Anschicks: pages 20, 21[3], 100, 108, 109, 151, 154[2], 160
Marlene Borneman: authors' photo, back flap
All historic photos: used by permission of the CMC

Albert Bierstadt painting, page 28-29:
BIERSTADT, Albert:
A Storm in the Rocky Mountains–Mount Rosalie. 1866.
Oil on canvas, 83 x 142¼" (210.8 x 361.3 cm).
Brooklyn Museum of Art. 76.79. Dick S. Ramsay Fund, Healy Purchase Fund B, Frank L. Babbott Fund, A. Augustus Healy Fund, Ella C. Woodward Memorial Fund, funds given by Daniel M. Kelly and Charles Simon, Carll H. de Silver Fund, Charles Stewart Smith Memorial Fund, Caroline A.L. Pratt Fund, Frederick Loeser Fund, Augustus Graham School of Design Fund, Museum Collection Fund, Special Subscription Fund, and the John B. Woodward Memorial Fund, Bequest of Mrs. William T. Brewster, Gift of Mrs. W. Woodward Phelps in memory of her mother and father, Ella M. and John C. Southwick, Gift of Seymour Barnard, Bequest of Laura L. Barnes, Gift of J.A.H. Bell, Bequest of Mark Finley, by exchange.

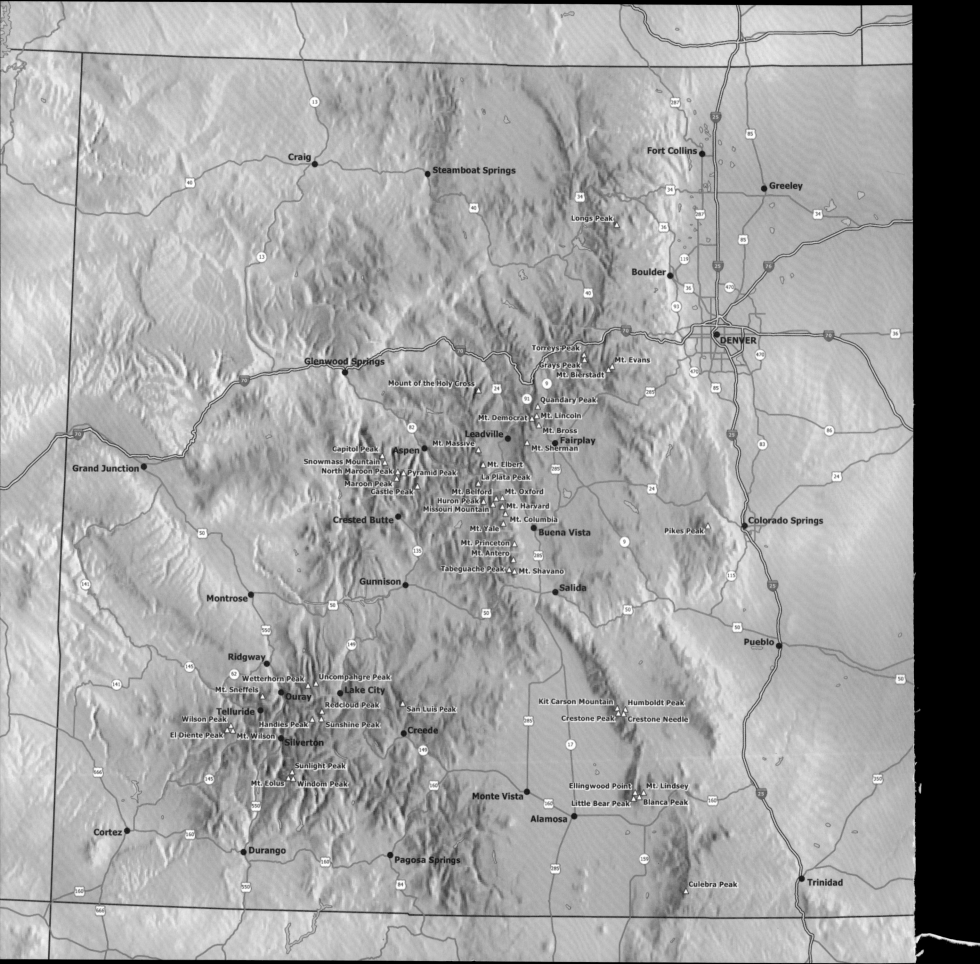